RV MAINTENANCE LOG BOOK

VEHICLE INFORMATION

VEHICLE INFORMATION

Make	
Model	
License Plate	

Owners Name	
Owners Address	
Owners Phone No	

Insurance Company	
Policy No	
Phone No	

Tow Capacity	
Tire Pressure	
Tank Capacity - Fresh	
Tank Capacity - Gray	
Tank Capacity - Propane	

MAINTENANCE CHECKLIST

Date: _____

- ○ Oil Change
- ○ Oil Filter
- ○ Air Filter
- ○ Fuel Filter
- ○ Fan Belts
- ○ Radiator Hose
- ○ Water Pump
- ○ Fluid Levels
- ○ Chassis
- ○ Tires
- ○ Wipers
- ○ A/C
- ○ Lights
- ○ Battery
- ○ Dump Valve
- ○ Black Tank
- ○ Gray Tank
- ○ Window Seals
- ○ Steps
- ○ Converter
- ○ Roof A/C

- ○ Propane Tank
- ○ Generator
- ○ Fresh Water Tank
- ○ Water Heater
- ○ Stove
- ○ Refrigerator
- ○ Furnace
- ○ Fire Extinguisher
- ○ Slide Seals
- ○ Frame
- ○ Locks
- ○ Latches
- ○ Trailer Brakes
- ○ Exterior Lights
- ○ Interior Lights
- ○ Tow Coupler
- ○ Breakaway Switch
- ○ _____
- ○ _____
- ○ _____
- ○ _____

Notes: _____

_____

_____

MAINTENANCE NOTES

Date:

MAINTENANCE CHECKLIST

Date: _____

- ○ Oil Change
- ○ Oil Filter
- ○ Air Filter
- ○ Fuel Filter
- ○ Fan Belts
- ○ Radiator Hose
- ○ Water Pump
- ○ Fluid Levels
- ○ Chassis
- ○ Tires
- ○ Wipers
- ○ A/C
- ○ Lights
- ○ Battery
- ○ Dump Valve
- ○ Black Tank
- ○ Gray Tank
- ○ Window Seals
- ○ Steps
- ○ Converter
- ○ Roof A/C

- ○ Propane Tank
- ○ Generator
- ○ Fresh Water Tank
- ○ Water Heater
- ○ Stove
- ○ Refrigerator
- ○ Furnace
- ○ Fire Extinguisher
- ○ Slide Seals
- ○ Frame
- ○ Locks
- ○ Latches
- ○ Trailer Brakes
- ○ Exterior Lights
- ○ Interior Lights
- ○ Tow Coupler
- ○ Breakaway Switch
- ○ _____
- ○ _____
- ○ _____
- ○ _____

Notes: _____

_____

_____

MAINTENANCE NOTES

Date:

MAINTENANCE CHECKLIST

Date: _____

- ○ Oil Change
- ○ Oil Filter
- ○ Air Filter
- ○ Fuel Filter
- ○ Fan Belts
- ○ Radiator Hose
- ○ Water Pump
- ○ Fluid Levels
- ○ Chassis
- ○ Tires
- ○ Wipers
- ○ A/C
- ○ Lights
- ○ Battery
- ○ Dump Valve
- ○ Black Tank
- ○ Gray Tank
- ○ Window Seals
- ○ Steps
- ○ Converter
- ○ Roof A/C

- ○ Propane Tank
- ○ Generator
- ○ Fresh Water Tank
- ○ Water Heater
- ○ Stove
- ○ Refrigerator
- ○ Furnace
- ○ Fire Extinguisher
- ○ Slide Seals
- ○ Frame
- ○ Locks
- ○ Latches
- ○ Trailer Brakes
- ○ Exterior Lights
- ○ Interior Lights
- ○ Tow Coupler
- ○ Breakaway Switch
- ○ _____
- ○ _____
- ○ _____
- ○ _____

Notes: _____

_____

_____

MAINTENANCE NOTES

Date:

MAINTENANCE CHECKLIST

Date: _____

- ○ Oil Change
- ○ Oil Filter
- ○ Air Filter
- ○ Fuel Filter
- ○ Fan Belts
- ○ Radiator Hose
- ○ Water Pump
- ○ Fluid Levels
- ○ Chassis
- ○ Tires
- ○ Wipers
- ○ A/C
- ○ Lights
- ○ Battery
- ○ Dump Valve
- ○ Black Tank
- ○ Gray Tank
- ○ Window Seals
- ○ Steps
- ○ Converter
- ○ Roof A/C

- ○ Propane Tank
- ○ Generator
- ○ Fresh Water Tank
- ○ Water Heater
- ○ Stove
- ○ Refrigerator
- ○ Furnace
- ○ Fire Extinguisher
- ○ Slide Seals
- ○ Frame
- ○ Locks
- ○ Latches
- ○ Trailer Brakes
- ○ Exterior Lights
- ○ Interior Lights
- ○ Tow Coupler
- ○ Breakaway Switch
- ○ _____
- ○ _____
- ○ _____
- ○ _____

Notes: _____

_____

_____

MAINTENANCE NOTES

Date:

MAINTENANCE CHECKLIST

Date: _____

- ○ Oil Change
- ○ Oil Filter
- ○ Air Filter
- ○ Fuel Filter
- ○ Fan Belts
- ○ Radiator Hose
- ○ Water Pump
- ○ Fluid Levels
- ○ Chassis
- ○ Tires
- ○ Wipers
- ○ A/C
- ○ Lights
- ○ Battery
- ○ Dump Valve
- ○ Black Tank
- ○ Gray Tank
- ○ Window Seals
- ○ Steps
- ○ Converter
- ○ Roof A/C

- ○ Propane Tank
- ○ Generator
- ○ Fresh Water Tank
- ○ Water Heater
- ○ Stove
- ○ Refrigerator
- ○ Furnace
- ○ Fire Extinguisher
- ○ Slide Seals
- ○ Frame
- ○ Locks
- ○ Latches
- ○ Trailer Brakes
- ○ Exterior Lights
- ○ Interior Lights
- ○ Tow Coupler
- ○ Breakaway Switch
- ○ _____
- ○ _____
- ○ _____
- ○ _____

Notes: _____

_____

_____

MAINTENANCE NOTES

Date:

MAINTENANCE CHECKLIST

Date: _____

- ○ Oil Change
- ○ Oil Filter
- ○ Air Filter
- ○ Fuel Filter
- ○ Fan Belts
- ○ Radiator Hose
- ○ Water Pump
- ○ Fluid Levels
- ○ Chassis
- ○ Tires
- ○ Wipers
- ○ A/C
- ○ Lights
- ○ Battery
- ○ Dump Valve
- ○ Black Tank
- ○ Gray Tank
- ○ Window Seals
- ○ Steps
- ○ Converter
- ○ Roof A/C

- ○ Propane Tank
- ○ Generator
- ○ Fresh Water Tank
- ○ Water Heater
- ○ Stove
- ○ Refrigerator
- ○ Furnace
- ○ Fire Extinguisher
- ○ Slide Seals
- ○ Frame
- ○ Locks
- ○ Latches
- ○ Trailer Brakes
- ○ Exterior Lights
- ○ Interior Lights
- ○ Tow Coupler
- ○ Breakaway Switch
- ○ _____
- ○ _____
- ○ _____
- ○ _____

Notes: _____

_____

_____

MAINTENANCE NOTES

Date:

MAINTENANCE CHECKLIST

Date: _____

- ○ Oil Change
- ○ Oil Filter
- ○ Air Filter
- ○ Fuel Filter
- ○ Fan Belts
- ○ Radiator Hose
- ○ Water Pump
- ○ Fluid Levels
- ○ Chassis
- ○ Tires
- ○ Wipers
- ○ A/C
- ○ Lights
- ○ Battery
- ○ Dump Valve
- ○ Black Tank
- ○ Gray Tank
- ○ Window Seals
- ○ Steps
- ○ Converter
- ○ Roof A/C

- ○ Propane Tank
- ○ Generator
- ○ Fresh Water Tank
- ○ Water Heater
- ○ Stove
- ○ Refrigerator
- ○ Furnace
- ○ Fire Extinguisher
- ○ Slide Seals
- ○ Frame
- ○ Locks
- ○ Latches
- ○ Trailer Brakes
- ○ Exterior Lights
- ○ Interior Lights
- ○ Tow Coupler
- ○ Breakaway Switch
- ○ _____
- ○ _____
- ○ _____
- ○ _____

Notes: _____

_____

_____

MAINTENANCE NOTES

Date:

MAINTENANCE CHECKLIST

Date: _____

- ○ Oil Change
- ○ Oil Filter
- ○ Air Filter
- ○ Fuel Filter
- ○ Fan Belts
- ○ Radiator Hose
- ○ Water Pump
- ○ Fluid Levels
- ○ Chassis
- ○ Tires
- ○ Wipers
- ○ A/C
- ○ Lights
- ○ Battery
- ○ Dump Valve
- ○ Black Tank
- ○ Gray Tank
- ○ Window Seals
- ○ Steps
- ○ Converter
- ○ Roof A/C

- ○ Propane Tank
- ○ Generator
- ○ Fresh Water Tank
- ○ Water Heater
- ○ Stove
- ○ Refrigerator
- ○ Furnace
- ○ Fire Extinguisher
- ○ Slide Seals
- ○ Frame
- ○ Locks
- ○ Latches
- ○ Trailer Brakes
- ○ Exterior Lights
- ○ Interior Lights
- ○ Tow Coupler
- ○ Breakaway Switch
- ○ _____
- ○ _____
- ○ _____
- ○ _____

Notes: _____

_____

_____

MAINTENANCE NOTES

Date:

MAINTENANCE CHECKLIST

Date: _____

- ○ Oil Change
- ○ Oil Filter
- ○ Air Filter
- ○ Fuel Filter
- ○ Fan Belts
- ○ Radiator Hose
- ○ Water Pump
- ○ Fluid Levels
- ○ Chassis
- ○ Tires
- ○ Wipers
- ○ A/C
- ○ Lights
- ○ Battery
- ○ Dump Valve
- ○ Black Tank
- ○ Gray Tank
- ○ Window Seals
- ○ Steps
- ○ Converter
- ○ Roof A/C

- ○ Propane Tank
- ○ Generator
- ○ Fresh Water Tank
- ○ Water Heater
- ○ Stove
- ○ Refrigerator
- ○ Furnace
- ○ Fire Extinguisher
- ○ Slide Seals
- ○ Frame
- ○ Locks
- ○ Latches
- ○ Trailer Brakes
- ○ Exterior Lights
- ○ Interior Lights
- ○ Tow Coupler
- ○ Breakaway Switch
- ○ _____
- ○ _____
- ○ _____
- ○ _____

Notes: _____

_____

_____

MAINTENANCE NOTES

ate:

MAINTENANCE CHECKLIST

Date: _____

- ○ Oil Change
- ○ Oil Filter
- ○ Air Filter
- ○ Fuel Filter
- ○ Fan Belts
- ○ Radiator Hose
- ○ Water Pump
- ○ Fluid Levels
- ○ Chassis
- ○ Tires
- ○ Wipers
- ○ A/C
- ○ Lights
- ○ Battery
- ○ Dump Valve
- ○ Black Tank
- ○ Gray Tank
- ○ Window Seals
- ○ Steps
- ○ Converter
- ○ Roof A/C

- ○ Propane Tank
- ○ Generator
- ○ Fresh Water Tank
- ○ Water Heater
- ○ Stove
- ○ Refrigerator
- ○ Furnace
- ○ Fire Extinguisher
- ○ Slide Seals
- ○ Frame
- ○ Locks
- ○ Latches
- ○ Trailer Brakes
- ○ Exterior Lights
- ○ Interior Lights
- ○ Tow Coupler
- ○ Breakaway Switch
- ○ _____
- ○ _____
- ○ _____
- ○ _____

Notes: _____

_____

_____

MAINTENANCE NOTES

Date:

MAINTENANCE CHECKLIST

Date: _____

- ○ Oil Change
- ○ Oil Filter
- ○ Air Filter
- ○ Fuel Filter
- ○ Fan Belts
- ○ Radiator Hose
- ○ Water Pump
- ○ Fluid Levels
- ○ Chassis
- ○ Tires
- ○ Wipers
- ○ A/C
- ○ Lights
- ○ Battery
- ○ Dump Valve
- ○ Black Tank
- ○ Gray Tank
- ○ Window Seals
- ○ Steps
- ○ Converter
- ○ Roof A/C

- ○ Propane Tank
- ○ Generator
- ○ Fresh Water Tank
- ○ Water Heater
- ○ Stove
- ○ Refrigerator
- ○ Furnace
- ○ Fire Extinguisher
- ○ Slide Seals
- ○ Frame
- ○ Locks
- ○ Latches
- ○ Trailer Brakes
- ○ Exterior Lights
- ○ Interior Lights
- ○ Tow Coupler
- ○ Breakaway Switch
- ○ _____
- ○ _____
- ○ _____
- ○ _____

Notes: _____

_____

_____

MAINTENANCE NOTES

ate:

MAINTENANCE CHECKLIST

Date: _____

- ○ Oil Change
- ○ Oil Filter
- ○ Air Filter
- ○ Fuel Filter
- ○ Fan Belts
- ○ Radiator Hose
- ○ Water Pump
- ○ Fluid Levels
- ○ Chassis
- ○ Tires
- ○ Wipers
- ○ A/C
- ○ Lights
- ○ Battery
- ○ Dump Valve
- ○ Black Tank
- ○ Gray Tank
- ○ Window Seals
- ○ Steps
- ○ Converter
- ○ Roof A/C

- ○ Propane Tank
- ○ Generator
- ○ Fresh Water Tank
- ○ Water Heater
- ○ Stove
- ○ Refrigerator
- ○ Furnace
- ○ Fire Extinguisher
- ○ Slide Seals
- ○ Frame
- ○ Locks
- ○ Latches
- ○ Trailer Brakes
- ○ Exterior Lights
- ○ Interior Lights
- ○ Tow Coupler
- ○ Breakaway Switch
- ○ _____
- ○ _____
- ○ _____
- ○ _____

Notes: _____

_____

_____

MAINTENANCE NOTES

Date:

MAINTENANCE CHECKLIST

Date: _____

- o Oil Change
- o Oil Filter
- o Air Filter
- o Fuel Filter
- o Fan Belts
- o Radiator Hose
- o Water Pump
- o Fluid Levels
- o Chassis
- o Tires
- o Wipers
- o A/C
- o Lights
- o Battery
- o Dump Valve
- o Black Tank
- o Gray Tank
- o Window Seals
- o Steps
- o Converter
- o Roof A/C

- o Propane Tank
- o Generator
- o Fresh Water Tank
- o Water Heater
- o Stove
- o Refrigerator
- o Furnace
- o Fire Extinguisher
- o Slide Seals
- o Frame
- o Locks
- o Latches
- o Trailer Brakes
- o Exterior Lights
- o Interior Lights
- o Tow Coupler
- o Breakaway Switch
- o _____
- o _____
- o _____
- o _____

Notes: _____

_____

_____

MAINTENANCE NOTES

ate:

MAINTENANCE CHECKLIST

Date: _____

- ○ Oil Change
- ○ Oil Filter
- ○ Air Filter
- ○ Fuel Filter
- ○ Fan Belts
- ○ Radiator Hose
- ○ Water Pump
- ○ Fluid Levels
- ○ Chassis
- ○ Tires
- ○ Wipers
- ○ A/C
- ○ Lights
- ○ Battery
- ○ Dump Valve
- ○ Black Tank
- ○ Gray Tank
- ○ Window Seals
- ○ Steps
- ○ Converter
- ○ Roof A/C

- ○ Propane Tank
- ○ Generator
- ○ Fresh Water Tank
- ○ Water Heater
- ○ Stove
- ○ Refrigerator
- ○ Furnace
- ○ Fire Extinguisher
- ○ Slide Seals
- ○ Frame
- ○ Locks
- ○ Latches
- ○ Trailer Brakes
- ○ Exterior Lights
- ○ Interior Lights
- ○ Tow Coupler
- ○ Breakaway Switch
- ○ _____
- ○ _____
- ○ _____
- ○ _____

Notes: _____

_____

_____

MAINTENANCE NOTES

Date:

MAINTENANCE CHECKLIST

Date: _____

○ Oil Change	○ Propane Tank
○ Oil Filter	○ Generator
○ Air Filter	○ Fresh Water Tank
○ Fuel Filter	○ Water Heater
○ Fan Belts	○ Stove
○ Radiator Hose	○ Refrigerator
○ Water Pump	○ Furnace
○ Fluid Levels	○ Fire Extinguisher
○ Chassis	○ Slide Seals
○ Tires	○ Frame
○ Wipers	○ Locks
○ A/C	○ Latches
○ Lights	○ Trailer Brakes
○ Battery	○ Exterior Lights
○ Dump Valve	○ Interior Lights
○ Black Tank	○ Tow Coupler
○ Gray Tank	○ Breakaway Switch
○ Window Seals	○ _____
○ Steps	○ _____
○ Converter	○ _____
○ Roof A/C	○ _____

Notes: _____

_____

_____

MAINTENANCE NOTES

Date:

MAINTENANCE CHECKLIST

Date: _____

- ○ Oil Change
- ○ Oil Filter
- ○ Air Filter
- ○ Fuel Filter
- ○ Fan Belts
- ○ Radiator Hose
- ○ Water Pump
- ○ Fluid Levels
- ○ Chassis
- ○ Tires
- ○ Wipers
- ○ A/C
- ○ Lights
- ○ Battery
- ○ Dump Valve
- ○ Black Tank
- ○ Gray Tank
- ○ Window Seals
- ○ Steps
- ○ Converter
- ○ Roof A/C

- ○ Propane Tank
- ○ Generator
- ○ Fresh Water Tank
- ○ Water Heater
- ○ Stove
- ○ Refrigerator
- ○ Furnace
- ○ Fire Extinguisher
- ○ Slide Seals
- ○ Frame
- ○ Locks
- ○ Latches
- ○ Trailer Brakes
- ○ Exterior Lights
- ○ Interior Lights
- ○ Tow Coupler
- ○ Breakaway Switch
- ○ _____
- ○ _____
- ○ _____
- ○ _____

Notes: _____

_____

_____

MAINTENANCE NOTES

Date:

MAINTENANCE CHECKLIST

Date: _____

- o Oil Change
- o Oil Filter
- o Air Filter
- o Fuel Filter
- o Fan Belts
- o Radiator Hose
- o Water Pump
- o Fluid Levels
- o Chassis
- o Tires
- o Wipers
- o A/C
- o Lights
- o Battery
- o Dump Valve
- o Black Tank
- o Gray Tank
- o Window Seals
- o Steps
- o Converter
- o Roof A/C

- o Propane Tank
- o Generator
- o Fresh Water Tank
- o Water Heater
- o Stove
- o Refrigerator
- o Furnace
- o Fire Extinguisher
- o Slide Seals
- o Frame
- o Locks
- o Latches
- o Trailer Brakes
- o Exterior Lights
- o Interior Lights
- o Tow Coupler
- o Breakaway Switch
- o _____
- o _____
- o _____
- o _____

Notes: _____

_____

_____

MAINTENANCE NOTES

Date:

MAINTENANCE CHECKLIST

Date: _____

- Oil Change
- Oil Filter
- Air Filter
- Fuel Filter
- Fan Belts
- Radiator Hose
- Water Pump
- Fluid Levels
- Chassis
- Tires
- Wipers
- A/C
- Lights
- Battery
- Dump Valve
- Black Tank
- Gray Tank
- Window Seals
- Steps
- Converter
- Roof A/C

- Propane Tank
- Generator
- Fresh Water Tank
- Water Heater
- Stove
- Refrigerator
- Furnace
- Fire Extinguisher
- Slide Seals
- Frame
- Locks
- Latches
- Trailer Brakes
- Exterior Lights
- Interior Lights
- Tow Coupler
- Breakaway Switch
- _____
- _____
- _____
- _____

Notes: _____

_____

_____

MAINTENANCE NOTES

Date:

MAINTENANCE CHECKLIST

Date: _____

- ○ Oil Change
- ○ Oil Filter
- ○ Air Filter
- ○ Fuel Filter
- ○ Fan Belts
- ○ Radiator Hose
- ○ Water Pump
- ○ Fluid Levels
- ○ Chassis
- ○ Tires
- ○ Wipers
- ○ A/C
- ○ Lights
- ○ Battery
- ○ Dump Valve
- ○ Black Tank
- ○ Gray Tank
- ○ Window Seals
- ○ Steps
- ○ Converter
- ○ Roof A/C

- ○ Propane Tank
- ○ Generator
- ○ Fresh Water Tank
- ○ Water Heater
- ○ Stove
- ○ Refrigerator
- ○ Furnace
- ○ Fire Extinguisher
- ○ Slide Seals
- ○ Frame
- ○ Locks
- ○ Latches
- ○ Trailer Brakes
- ○ Exterior Lights
- ○ Interior Lights
- ○ Tow Coupler
- ○ Breakaway Switch
- ○ _____
- ○ _____
- ○ _____
- ○ _____

Notes: _____

_____

_____

MAINTENANCE NOTES

Date:

MAINTENANCE CHECKLIST

Date: _____

- ○ Oil Change
- ○ Oil Filter
- ○ Air Filter
- ○ Fuel Filter
- ○ Fan Belts
- ○ Radiator Hose
- ○ Water Pump
- ○ Fluid Levels
- ○ Chassis
- ○ Tires
- ○ Wipers
- ○ A/C
- ○ Lights
- ○ Battery
- ○ Dump Valve
- ○ Black Tank
- ○ Gray Tank
- ○ Window Seals
- ○ Steps
- ○ Converter
- ○ Roof A/C

- ○ Propane Tank
- ○ Generator
- ○ Fresh Water Tank
- ○ Water Heater
- ○ Stove
- ○ Refrigerator
- ○ Furnace
- ○ Fire Extinguisher
- ○ Slide Seals
- ○ Frame
- ○ Locks
- ○ Latches
- ○ Trailer Brakes
- ○ Exterior Lights
- ○ Interior Lights
- ○ Tow Coupler
- ○ Breakaway Switch
- ○ _____
- ○ _____
- ○ _____
- ○ _____

Notes: _____

_____

_____

MAINTENANCE NOTES

ate:

MAINTENANCE CHECKLIST

Date: _____

○ Oil Change	○ Propane Tank
○ Oil Filter	○ Generator
○ Air Filter	○ Fresh Water Tank
○ Fuel Filter	○ Water Heater
○ Fan Belts	○ Stove
○ Radiator Hose	○ Refrigerator
○ Water Pump	○ Furnace
○ Fluid Levels	○ Fire Extinguisher
○ Chassis	○ Slide Seals
○ Tires	○ Frame
○ Wipers	○ Locks
○ A/C	○ Latches
○ Lights	○ Trailer Brakes
○ Battery	○ Exterior Lights
○ Dump Valve	○ Interior Lights
○ Black Tank	○ Tow Coupler
○ Gray Tank	○ Breakaway Switch
○ Window Seals	○ _____
○ Steps	○ _____
○ Converter	○ _____
○ Roof A/C	○ _____

Notes: _____

_____

_____

MAINTENANCE NOTES

Date:

MAINTENANCE CHECKLIST

Date: _____

- ○ Oil Change
- ○ Oil Filter
- ○ Air Filter
- ○ Fuel Filter
- ○ Fan Belts
- ○ Radiator Hose
- ○ Water Pump
- ○ Fluid Levels
- ○ Chassis
- ○ Tires
- ○ Wipers
- ○ A/C
- ○ Lights
- ○ Battery
- ○ Dump Valve
- ○ Black Tank
- ○ Gray Tank
- ○ Window Seals
- ○ Steps
- ○ Converter
- ○ Roof A/C

- ○ Propane Tank
- ○ Generator
- ○ Fresh Water Tank
- ○ Water Heater
- ○ Stove
- ○ Refrigerator
- ○ Furnace
- ○ Fire Extinguisher
- ○ Slide Seals
- ○ Frame
- ○ Locks
- ○ Latches
- ○ Trailer Brakes
- ○ Exterior Lights
- ○ Interior Lights
- ○ Tow Coupler
- ○ Breakaway Switch
- ○ _____
- ○ _____
- ○ _____
- ○ _____

Notes: _____

_____

_____

MAINTENANCE NOTES

Date:

MAINTENANCE CHECKLIST

Date: _____

- ○ Oil Change
- ○ Oil Filter
- ○ Air Filter
- ○ Fuel Filter
- ○ Fan Belts
- ○ Radiator Hose
- ○ Water Pump
- ○ Fluid Levels
- ○ Chassis
- ○ Tires
- ○ Wipers
- ○ A/C
- ○ Lights
- ○ Battery
- ○ Dump Valve
- ○ Black Tank
- ○ Gray Tank
- ○ Window Seals
- ○ Steps
- ○ Converter
- ○ Roof A/C

- ○ Propane Tank
- ○ Generator
- ○ Fresh Water Tank
- ○ Water Heater
- ○ Stove
- ○ Refrigerator
- ○ Furnace
- ○ Fire Extinguisher
- ○ Slide Seals
- ○ Frame
- ○ Locks
- ○ Latches
- ○ Trailer Brakes
- ○ Exterior Lights
- ○ Interior Lights
- ○ Tow Coupler
- ○ Breakaway Switch
- ○ _____
- ○ _____
- ○ _____
- ○ _____

Notes: _____

_____

_____

MAINTENANCE NOTES

Date:

MAINTENANCE CHECKLIST

Date: _____

- ○ Oil Change
- ○ Oil Filter
- ○ Air Filter
- ○ Fuel Filter
- ○ Fan Belts
- ○ Radiator Hose
- ○ Water Pump
- ○ Fluid Levels
- ○ Chassis
- ○ Tires
- ○ Wipers
- ○ A/C
- ○ Lights
- ○ Battery
- ○ Dump Valve
- ○ Black Tank
- ○ Gray Tank
- ○ Window Seals
- ○ Steps
- ○ Converter
- ○ Roof A/C

- ○ Propane Tank
- ○ Generator
- ○ Fresh Water Tank
- ○ Water Heater
- ○ Stove
- ○ Refrigerator
- ○ Furnace
- ○ Fire Extinguisher
- ○ Slide Seals
- ○ Frame
- ○ Locks
- ○ Latches
- ○ Trailer Brakes
- ○ Exterior Lights
- ○ Interior Lights
- ○ Tow Coupler
- ○ Breakaway Switch
- ○ _____
- ○ _____
- ○ _____
- ○ _____

Notes: _____

_____

_____

MAINTENANCE NOTES

ate:

MAINTENANCE CHECKLIST

Date: _____

- ○ Oil Change
- ○ Oil Filter
- ○ Air Filter
- ○ Fuel Filter
- ○ Fan Belts
- ○ Radiator Hose
- ○ Water Pump
- ○ Fluid Levels
- ○ Chassis
- ○ Tires
- ○ Wipers
- ○ A/C
- ○ Lights
- ○ Battery
- ○ Dump Valve
- ○ Black Tank
- ○ Gray Tank
- ○ Window Seals
- ○ Steps
- ○ Converter
- ○ Roof A/C

- ○ Propane Tank
- ○ Generator
- ○ Fresh Water Tank
- ○ Water Heater
- ○ Stove
- ○ Refrigerator
- ○ Furnace
- ○ Fire Extinguisher
- ○ Slide Seals
- ○ Frame
- ○ Locks
- ○ Latches
- ○ Trailer Brakes
- ○ Exterior Lights
- ○ Interior Lights
- ○ Tow Coupler
- ○ Breakaway Switch
- ○ _____
- ○ _____
- ○ _____
- ○ _____

Notes: _____

_____

_____

MAINTENANCE NOTES

ate:

MAINTENANCE CHECKLIST

Date: _____

- ○ Oil Change
- ○ Oil Filter
- ○ Air Filter
- ○ Fuel Filter
- ○ Fan Belts
- ○ Radiator Hose
- ○ Water Pump
- ○ Fluid Levels
- ○ Chassis
- ○ Tires
- ○ Wipers
- ○ A/C
- ○ Lights
- ○ Battery
- ○ Dump Valve
- ○ Black Tank
- ○ Gray Tank
- ○ Window Seals
- ○ Steps
- ○ Converter
- ○ Roof A/C

- ○ Propane Tank
- ○ Generator
- ○ Fresh Water Tank
- ○ Water Heater
- ○ Stove
- ○ Refrigerator
- ○ Furnace
- ○ Fire Extinguisher
- ○ Slide Seals
- ○ Frame
- ○ Locks
- ○ Latches
- ○ Trailer Brakes
- ○ Exterior Lights
- ○ Interior Lights
- ○ Tow Coupler
- ○ Breakaway Switch
- ○ _____
- ○ _____
- ○ _____
- ○ _____

Notes: _____
_____
_____

MAINTENANCE NOTES

ate:

MAINTENANCE CHECKLIST

Date: _____

- ○ Oil Change
- ○ Oil Filter
- ○ Air Filter
- ○ Fuel Filter
- ○ Fan Belts
- ○ Radiator Hose
- ○ Water Pump
- ○ Fluid Levels
- ○ Chassis
- ○ Tires
- ○ Wipers
- ○ A/C
- ○ Lights
- ○ Battery
- ○ Dump Valve
- ○ Black Tank
- ○ Gray Tank
- ○ Window Seals
- ○ Steps
- ○ Converter
- ○ Roof A/C

- ○ Propane Tank
- ○ Generator
- ○ Fresh Water Tank
- ○ Water Heater
- ○ Stove
- ○ Refrigerator
- ○ Furnace
- ○ Fire Extinguisher
- ○ Slide Seals
- ○ Frame
- ○ Locks
- ○ Latches
- ○ Trailer Brakes
- ○ Exterior Lights
- ○ Interior Lights
- ○ Tow Coupler
- ○ Breakaway Switch
- ○ _____
- ○ _____
- ○ _____
- ○ _____

Notes: _____

_____

_____

MAINTENANCE NOTES

Date:

MAINTENANCE CHECKLIST

Date: _____

- ○ Oil Change
- ○ Oil Filter
- ○ Air Filter
- ○ Fuel Filter
- ○ Fan Belts
- ○ Radiator Hose
- ○ Water Pump
- ○ Fluid Levels
- ○ Chassis
- ○ Tires
- ○ Wipers
- ○ A/C
- ○ Lights
- ○ Battery
- ○ Dump Valve
- ○ Black Tank
- ○ Gray Tank
- ○ Window Seals
- ○ Steps
- ○ Converter
- ○ Roof A/C

- ○ Propane Tank
- ○ Generator
- ○ Fresh Water Tank
- ○ Water Heater
- ○ Stove
- ○ Refrigerator
- ○ Furnace
- ○ Fire Extinguisher
- ○ Slide Seals
- ○ Frame
- ○ Locks
- ○ Latches
- ○ Trailer Brakes
- ○ Exterior Lights
- ○ Interior Lights
- ○ Tow Coupler
- ○ Breakaway Switch
- ○ _____
- ○ _____
- ○ _____
- ○ _____

Notes: _____

_____

_____

MAINTENANCE NOTES

ate:

MAINTENANCE CHECKLIST

Date: _____

- ○ Oil Change
- ○ Oil Filter
- ○ Air Filter
- ○ Fuel Filter
- ○ Fan Belts
- ○ Radiator Hose
- ○ Water Pump
- ○ Fluid Levels
- ○ Chassis
- ○ Tires
- ○ Wipers
- ○ A/C
- ○ Lights
- ○ Battery
- ○ Dump Valve
- ○ Black Tank
- ○ Gray Tank
- ○ Window Seals
- ○ Steps
- ○ Converter
- ○ Roof A/C

- ○ Propane Tank
- ○ Generator
- ○ Fresh Water Tank
- ○ Water Heater
- ○ Stove
- ○ Refrigerator
- ○ Furnace
- ○ Fire Extinguisher
- ○ Slide Seals
- ○ Frame
- ○ Locks
- ○ Latches
- ○ Trailer Brakes
- ○ Exterior Lights
- ○ Interior Lights
- ○ Tow Coupler
- ○ Breakaway Switch
- ○ _____
- ○ _____
- ○ _____
- ○ _____

Notes: _____

_____

_____

MAINTENANCE NOTES

ate:

MAINTENANCE CHECKLIST

Date: _____

- ○ Oil Change
- ○ Oil Filter
- ○ Air Filter
- ○ Fuel Filter
- ○ Fan Belts
- ○ Radiator Hose
- ○ Water Pump
- ○ Fluid Levels
- ○ Chassis
- ○ Tires
- ○ Wipers
- ○ A/C
- ○ Lights
- ○ Battery
- ○ Dump Valve
- ○ Black Tank
- ○ Gray Tank
- ○ Window Seals
- ○ Steps
- ○ Converter
- ○ Roof A/C

- ○ Propane Tank
- ○ Generator
- ○ Fresh Water Tank
- ○ Water Heater
- ○ Stove
- ○ Refrigerator
- ○ Furnace
- ○ Fire Extinguisher
- ○ Slide Seals
- ○ Frame
- ○ Locks
- ○ Latches
- ○ Trailer Brakes
- ○ Exterior Lights
- ○ Interior Lights
- ○ Tow Coupler
- ○ Breakaway Switch
- ○ _____
- ○ _____
- ○ _____
- ○ _____

Notes: _____

_____

_____

MAINTENANCE NOTES

Date:

MAINTENANCE CHECKLIST

Date: _____

- ○ Oil Change
- ○ Oil Filter
- ○ Air Filter
- ○ Fuel Filter
- ○ Fan Belts
- ○ Radiator Hose
- ○ Water Pump
- ○ Fluid Levels
- ○ Chassis
- ○ Tires
- ○ Wipers
- ○ A/C
- ○ Lights
- ○ Battery
- ○ Dump Valve
- ○ Black Tank
- ○ Gray Tank
- ○ Window Seals
- ○ Steps
- ○ Converter
- ○ Roof A/C

- ○ Propane Tank
- ○ Generator
- ○ Fresh Water Tank
- ○ Water Heater
- ○ Stove
- ○ Refrigerator
- ○ Furnace
- ○ Fire Extinguisher
- ○ Slide Seals
- ○ Frame
- ○ Locks
- ○ Latches
- ○ Trailer Brakes
- ○ Exterior Lights
- ○ Interior Lights
- ○ Tow Coupler
- ○ Breakaway Switch
- ○ _____
- ○ _____
- ○ _____
- ○ _____

Notes: _____

_____

_____

MAINTENANCE NOTES

Date:

MAINTENANCE CHECKLIST

Date: _____

○ Oil Change	○ Propane Tank
○ Oil Filter	○ Generator
○ Air Filter	○ Fresh Water Tank
○ Fuel Filter	○ Water Heater
○ Fan Belts	○ Stove
○ Radiator Hose	○ Refrigerator
○ Water Pump	○ Furnace
○ Fluid Levels	○ Fire Extinguisher
○ Chassis	○ Slide Seals
○ Tires	○ Frame
○ Wipers	○ Locks
○ A/C	○ Latches
○ Lights	○ Trailer Brakes
○ Battery	○ Exterior Lights
○ Dump Valve	○ Interior Lights
○ Black Tank	○ Tow Coupler
○ Gray Tank	○ Breakaway Switch
○ Window Seals	○ _____
○ Steps	○ _____
○ Converter	○ _____
○ Roof A/C	○ _____

Notes: _____

_____

_____

MAINTENANCE NOTES

ate:

MAINTENANCE CHECKLIST

Date: _____

- ○ Oil Change
- ○ Oil Filter
- ○ Air Filter
- ○ Fuel Filter
- ○ Fan Belts
- ○ Radiator Hose
- ○ Water Pump
- ○ Fluid Levels
- ○ Chassis
- ○ Tires
- ○ Wipers
- ○ A/C
- ○ Lights
- ○ Battery
- ○ Dump Valve
- ○ Black Tank
- ○ Gray Tank
- ○ Window Seals
- ○ Steps
- ○ Converter
- ○ Roof A/C

- ○ Propane Tank
- ○ Generator
- ○ Fresh Water Tank
- ○ Water Heater
- ○ Stove
- ○ Refrigerator
- ○ Furnace
- ○ Fire Extinguisher
- ○ Slide Seals
- ○ Frame
- ○ Locks
- ○ Latches
- ○ Trailer Brakes
- ○ Exterior Lights
- ○ Interior Lights
- ○ Tow Coupler
- ○ Breakaway Switch
- ○ _____
- ○ _____
- ○ _____
- ○ _____

Notes: _____

_____

_____

MAINTENANCE NOTES

Date:

MAINTENANCE CHECKLIST

Date: _____

- ○ Oil Change
- ○ Oil Filter
- ○ Air Filter
- ○ Fuel Filter
- ○ Fan Belts
- ○ Radiator Hose
- ○ Water Pump
- ○ Fluid Levels
- ○ Chassis
- ○ Tires
- ○ Wipers
- ○ A/C
- ○ Lights
- ○ Battery
- ○ Dump Valve
- ○ Black Tank
- ○ Gray Tank
- ○ Window Seals
- ○ Steps
- ○ Converter
- ○ Roof A/C

- ○ Propane Tank
- ○ Generator
- ○ Fresh Water Tank
- ○ Water Heater
- ○ Stove
- ○ Refrigerator
- ○ Furnace
- ○ Fire Extinguisher
- ○ Slide Seals
- ○ Frame
- ○ Locks
- ○ Latches
- ○ Trailer Brakes
- ○ Exterior Lights
- ○ Interior Lights
- ○ Tow Coupler
- ○ Breakaway Switch
- ○ _____
- ○ _____
- ○ _____
- ○ _____

Notes: _____

_____

_____

MAINTENANCE NOTES

ate:

MAINTENANCE CHECKLIST

Date: _____

o Oil Change	o Propane Tank
o Oil Filter	o Generator
o Air Filter	o Fresh Water Tank
o Fuel Filter	o Water Heater
o Fan Belts	o Stove
o Radiator Hose	o Refrigerator
o Water Pump	o Furnace
o Fluid Levels	o Fire Extinguisher
o Chassis	o Slide Seals
o Tires	o Frame
o Wipers	o Locks
o A/C	o Latches
o Lights	o Trailer Brakes
o Battery	o Exterior Lights
o Dump Valve	o Interior Lights
o Black Tank	o Tow Coupler
o Gray Tank	o Breakaway Switch
o Window Seals	o _____
o Steps	o _____
o Converter	o _____
o Roof A/C	o _____

Notes: _____

_____

_____

MAINTENANCE NOTES

Date:

MAINTENANCE CHECKLIST

Date: _____

- ○ Oil Change
- ○ Oil Filter
- ○ Air Filter
- ○ Fuel Filter
- ○ Fan Belts
- ○ Radiator Hose
- ○ Water Pump
- ○ Fluid Levels
- ○ Chassis
- ○ Tires
- ○ Wipers
- ○ A/C
- ○ Lights
- ○ Battery
- ○ Dump Valve
- ○ Black Tank
- ○ Gray Tank
- ○ Window Seals
- ○ Steps
- ○ Converter
- ○ Roof A/C

- ○ Propane Tank
- ○ Generator
- ○ Fresh Water Tank
- ○ Water Heater
- ○ Stove
- ○ Refrigerator
- ○ Furnace
- ○ Fire Extinguisher
- ○ Slide Seals
- ○ Frame
- ○ Locks
- ○ Latches
- ○ Trailer Brakes
- ○ Exterior Lights
- ○ Interior Lights
- ○ Tow Coupler
- ○ Breakaway Switch
- ○ _____
- ○ _____
- ○ _____
- ○ _____

Notes: _____

_____

_____

MAINTENANCE NOTES

ate:

MAINTENANCE CHECKLIST

Date: _____

- ○ Oil Change
- ○ Oil Filter
- ○ Air Filter
- ○ Fuel Filter
- ○ Fan Belts
- ○ Radiator Hose
- ○ Water Pump
- ○ Fluid Levels
- ○ Chassis
- ○ Tires
- ○ Wipers
- ○ A/C
- ○ Lights
- ○ Battery
- ○ Dump Valve
- ○ Black Tank
- ○ Gray Tank
- ○ Window Seals
- ○ Steps
- ○ Converter
- ○ Roof A/C

- ○ Propane Tank
- ○ Generator
- ○ Fresh Water Tank
- ○ Water Heater
- ○ Stove
- ○ Refrigerator
- ○ Furnace
- ○ Fire Extinguisher
- ○ Slide Seals
- ○ Frame
- ○ Locks
- ○ Latches
- ○ Trailer Brakes
- ○ Exterior Lights
- ○ Interior Lights
- ○ Tow Coupler
- ○ Breakaway Switch
- ○ _____
- ○ _____
- ○ _____
- ○ _____

Notes: _____

_____

_____

MAINTENANCE NOTES

Date:

MAINTENANCE CHECKLIST

Date: _____

- ○ Oil Change
- ○ Oil Filter
- ○ Air Filter
- ○ Fuel Filter
- ○ Fan Belts
- ○ Radiator Hose
- ○ Water Pump
- ○ Fluid Levels
- ○ Chassis
- ○ Tires
- ○ Wipers
- ○ A/C
- ○ Lights
- ○ Battery
- ○ Dump Valve
- ○ Black Tank
- ○ Gray Tank
- ○ Window Seals
- ○ Steps
- ○ Converter
- ○ Roof A/C

- ○ Propane Tank
- ○ Generator
- ○ Fresh Water Tank
- ○ Water Heater
- ○ Stove
- ○ Refrigerator
- ○ Furnace
- ○ Fire Extinguisher
- ○ Slide Seals
- ○ Frame
- ○ Locks
- ○ Latches
- ○ Trailer Brakes
- ○ Exterior Lights
- ○ Interior Lights
- ○ Tow Coupler
- ○ Breakaway Switch
- ○ _____
- ○ _____
- ○ _____
- ○ _____

Notes: _____

_____

_____

MAINTENANCE NOTES

ate:

MAINTENANCE CHECKLIST

Date: _____

- ○ Oil Change
- ○ Oil Filter
- ○ Air Filter
- ○ Fuel Filter
- ○ Fan Belts
- ○ Radiator Hose
- ○ Water Pump
- ○ Fluid Levels
- ○ Chassis
- ○ Tires
- ○ Wipers
- ○ A/C
- ○ Lights
- ○ Battery
- ○ Dump Valve
- ○ Black Tank
- ○ Gray Tank
- ○ Window Seals
- ○ Steps
- ○ Converter
- ○ Roof A/C

- ○ Propane Tank
- ○ Generator
- ○ Fresh Water Tank
- ○ Water Heater
- ○ Stove
- ○ Refrigerator
- ○ Furnace
- ○ Fire Extinguisher
- ○ Slide Seals
- ○ Frame
- ○ Locks
- ○ Latches
- ○ Trailer Brakes
- ○ Exterior Lights
- ○ Interior Lights
- ○ Tow Coupler
- ○ Breakaway Switch
- ○ _____
- ○ _____
- ○ _____
- ○ _____

Notes: _____

_____

_____

MAINTENANCE NOTES

ate:

MAINTENANCE CHECKLIST

Date: _____

- ○ Oil Change
- ○ Oil Filter
- ○ Air Filter
- ○ Fuel Filter
- ○ Fan Belts
- ○ Radiator Hose
- ○ Water Pump
- ○ Fluid Levels
- ○ Chassis
- ○ Tires
- ○ Wipers
- ○ A/C
- ○ Lights
- ○ Battery
- ○ Dump Valve
- ○ Black Tank
- ○ Gray Tank
- ○ Window Seals
- ○ Steps
- ○ Converter
- ○ Roof A/C

- ○ Propane Tank
- ○ Generator
- ○ Fresh Water Tank
- ○ Water Heater
- ○ Stove
- ○ Refrigerator
- ○ Furnace
- ○ Fire Extinguisher
- ○ Slide Seals
- ○ Frame
- ○ Locks
- ○ Latches
- ○ Trailer Brakes
- ○ Exterior Lights
- ○ Interior Lights
- ○ Tow Coupler
- ○ Breakaway Switch
- ○ _____
- ○ _____
- ○ _____
- ○ _____

Notes: _____

_____

_____

MAINTENANCE NOTES

ate:

MAINTENANCE CHECKLIST

Date: _____

- ○ Oil Change
- ○ Oil Filter
- ○ Air Filter
- ○ Fuel Filter
- ○ Fan Belts
- ○ Radiator Hose
- ○ Water Pump
- ○ Fluid Levels
- ○ Chassis
- ○ Tires
- ○ Wipers
- ○ A/C
- ○ Lights
- ○ Battery
- ○ Dump Valve
- ○ Black Tank
- ○ Gray Tank
- ○ Window Seals
- ○ Steps
- ○ Converter
- ○ Roof A/C

- ○ Propane Tank
- ○ Generator
- ○ Fresh Water Tank
- ○ Water Heater
- ○ Stove
- ○ Refrigerator
- ○ Furnace
- ○ Fire Extinguisher
- ○ Slide Seals
- ○ Frame
- ○ Locks
- ○ Latches
- ○ Trailer Brakes
- ○ Exterior Lights
- ○ Interior Lights
- ○ Tow Coupler
- ○ Breakaway Switch
- ○ _____
- ○ _____
- ○ _____
- ○ _____

Notes: _____

_____

_____

MAINTENANCE NOTES

ate:

MAINTENANCE CHECKLIST

Date: _____

- ○ Oil Change
- ○ Oil Filter
- ○ Air Filter
- ○ Fuel Filter
- ○ Fan Belts
- ○ Radiator Hose
- ○ Water Pump
- ○ Fluid Levels
- ○ Chassis
- ○ Tires
- ○ Wipers
- ○ A/C
- ○ Lights
- ○ Battery
- ○ Dump Valve
- ○ Black Tank
- ○ Gray Tank
- ○ Window Seals
- ○ Steps
- ○ Converter
- ○ Roof A/C

- ○ Propane Tank
- ○ Generator
- ○ Fresh Water Tank
- ○ Water Heater
- ○ Stove
- ○ Refrigerator
- ○ Furnace
- ○ Fire Extinguisher
- ○ Slide Seals
- ○ Frame
- ○ Locks
- ○ Latches
- ○ Trailer Brakes
- ○ Exterior Lights
- ○ Interior Lights
- ○ Tow Coupler
- ○ Breakaway Switch
- ○ _____
- ○ _____
- ○ _____
- ○ _____

Notes: _____

_____

_____

MAINTENANCE NOTES

ate:

MAINTENANCE CHECKLIST

Date: _____

- ○ Oil Change
- ○ Oil Filter
- ○ Air Filter
- ○ Fuel Filter
- ○ Fan Belts
- ○ Radiator Hose
- ○ Water Pump
- ○ Fluid Levels
- ○ Chassis
- ○ Tires
- ○ Wipers
- ○ A/C
- ○ Lights
- ○ Battery
- ○ Dump Valve
- ○ Black Tank
- ○ Gray Tank
- ○ Window Seals
- ○ Steps
- ○ Converter
- ○ Roof A/C

- ○ Propane Tank
- ○ Generator
- ○ Fresh Water Tank
- ○ Water Heater
- ○ Stove
- ○ Refrigerator
- ○ Furnace
- ○ Fire Extinguisher
- ○ Slide Seals
- ○ Frame
- ○ Locks
- ○ Latches
- ○ Trailer Brakes
- ○ Exterior Lights
- ○ Interior Lights
- ○ Tow Coupler
- ○ Breakaway Switch
- ○ _____
- ○ _____
- ○ _____
- ○ _____

Notes: _____

_____

_____

MAINTENANCE NOTES

ate:

MAINTENANCE CHECKLIST

Date: _____

- ○ Oil Change
- ○ Oil Filter
- ○ Air Filter
- ○ Fuel Filter
- ○ Fan Belts
- ○ Radiator Hose
- ○ Water Pump
- ○ Fluid Levels
- ○ Chassis
- ○ Tires
- ○ Wipers
- ○ A/C
- ○ Lights
- ○ Battery
- ○ Dump Valve
- ○ Black Tank
- ○ Gray Tank
- ○ Window Seals
- ○ Steps
- ○ Converter
- ○ Roof A/C

- ○ Propane Tank
- ○ Generator
- ○ Fresh Water Tank
- ○ Water Heater
- ○ Stove
- ○ Refrigerator
- ○ Furnace
- ○ Fire Extinguisher
- ○ Slide Seals
- ○ Frame
- ○ Locks
- ○ Latches
- ○ Trailer Brakes
- ○ Exterior Lights
- ○ Interior Lights
- ○ Tow Coupler
- ○ Breakaway Switch
- ○ _____
- ○ _____
- ○ _____
- ○ _____

Notes: _____

_____

_____

MAINTENANCE NOTES

Date:

MAINTENANCE CHECKLIST

Date: _____

- ○ Oil Change
- ○ Oil Filter
- ○ Air Filter
- ○ Fuel Filter
- ○ Fan Belts
- ○ Radiator Hose
- ○ Water Pump
- ○ Fluid Levels
- ○ Chassis
- ○ Tires
- ○ Wipers
- ○ A/C
- ○ Lights
- ○ Battery
- ○ Dump Valve
- ○ Black Tank
- ○ Gray Tank
- ○ Window Seals
- ○ Steps
- ○ Converter
- ○ Roof A/C

- ○ Propane Tank
- ○ Generator
- ○ Fresh Water Tank
- ○ Water Heater
- ○ Stove
- ○ Refrigerator
- ○ Furnace
- ○ Fire Extinguisher
- ○ Slide Seals
- ○ Frame
- ○ Locks
- ○ Latches
- ○ Trailer Brakes
- ○ Exterior Lights
- ○ Interior Lights
- ○ Tow Coupler
- ○ Breakaway Switch
- ○ _____
- ○ _____
- ○ _____
- ○ _____

Notes: _____

_____

_____

MAINTENANCE NOTES

Date:

MAINTENANCE CHECKLIST

Date: _____

- ○ Oil Change
- ○ Oil Filter
- ○ Air Filter
- ○ Fuel Filter
- ○ Fan Belts
- ○ Radiator Hose
- ○ Water Pump
- ○ Fluid Levels
- ○ Chassis
- ○ Tires
- ○ Wipers
- ○ A/C
- ○ Lights
- ○ Battery
- ○ Dump Valve
- ○ Black Tank
- ○ Gray Tank
- ○ Window Seals
- ○ Steps
- ○ Converter
- ○ Roof A/C

- ○ Propane Tank
- ○ Generator
- ○ Fresh Water Tank
- ○ Water Heater
- ○ Stove
- ○ Refrigerator
- ○ Furnace
- ○ Fire Extinguisher
- ○ Slide Seals
- ○ Frame
- ○ Locks
- ○ Latches
- ○ Trailer Brakes
- ○ Exterior Lights
- ○ Interior Lights
- ○ Tow Coupler
- ○ Breakaway Switch
- ○ _____
- ○ _____
- ○ _____
- ○ _____

Notes: _____

_____

_____

MAINTENANCE NOTES

Date:

MAINTENANCE CHECKLIST

Date: _____

○ Oil Change	○ Propane Tank
○ Oil Filter	○ Generator
○ Air Filter	○ Fresh Water Tank
○ Fuel Filter	○ Water Heater
○ Fan Belts	○ Stove
○ Radiator Hose	○ Refrigerator
○ Water Pump	○ Furnace
○ Fluid Levels	○ Fire Extinguisher
○ Chassis	○ Slide Seals
○ Tires	○ Frame
○ Wipers	○ Locks
○ A/C	○ Latches
○ Lights	○ Trailer Brakes
○ Battery	○ Exterior Lights
○ Dump Valve	○ Interior Lights
○ Black Tank	○ Tow Coupler
○ Gray Tank	○ Breakaway Switch
○ Window Seals	○ _____
○ Steps	○ _____
○ Converter	○ _____
○ Roof A/C	○ _____

Notes: _____

_____

_____

MAINTENANCE NOTES

Date:

MAINTENANCE CHECKLIST

Date: _____

- ○ Oil Change
- ○ Oil Filter
- ○ Air Filter
- ○ Fuel Filter
- ○ Fan Belts
- ○ Radiator Hose
- ○ Water Pump
- ○ Fluid Levels
- ○ Chassis
- ○ Tires
- ○ Wipers
- ○ A/C
- ○ Lights
- ○ Battery
- ○ Dump Valve
- ○ Black Tank
- ○ Gray Tank
- ○ Window Seals
- ○ Steps
- ○ Converter
- ○ Roof A/C

- ○ Propane Tank
- ○ Generator
- ○ Fresh Water Tank
- ○ Water Heater
- ○ Stove
- ○ Refrigerator
- ○ Furnace
- ○ Fire Extinguisher
- ○ Slide Seals
- ○ Frame
- ○ Locks
- ○ Latches
- ○ Trailer Brakes
- ○ Exterior Lights
- ○ Interior Lights
- ○ Tow Coupler
- ○ Breakaway Switch
- ○ _____
- ○ _____
- ○ _____
- ○ _____

Notes: _____

_____

_____

MAINTENANCE NOTES

Date:

MAINTENANCE CHECKLIST

Date: _____

- ○ Oil Change
- ○ Oil Filter
- ○ Air Filter
- ○ Fuel Filter
- ○ Fan Belts
- ○ Radiator Hose
- ○ Water Pump
- ○ Fluid Levels
- ○ Chassis
- ○ Tires
- ○ Wipers
- ○ A/C
- ○ Lights
- ○ Battery
- ○ Dump Valve
- ○ Black Tank
- ○ Gray Tank
- ○ Window Seals
- ○ Steps
- ○ Converter
- ○ Roof A/C

- ○ Propane Tank
- ○ Generator
- ○ Fresh Water Tank
- ○ Water Heater
- ○ Stove
- ○ Refrigerator
- ○ Furnace
- ○ Fire Extinguisher
- ○ Slide Seals
- ○ Frame
- ○ Locks
- ○ Latches
- ○ Trailer Brakes
- ○ Exterior Lights
- ○ Interior Lights
- ○ Tow Coupler
- ○ Breakaway Switch
- ○ _____
- ○ _____
- ○ _____
- ○ _____

Notes: _____

_____

_____

Made in United States
Orlando, FL
27 January 2022

14090605R00057